Electronic Keyboard
Grade 2

Pieces & Technical Work
for Trinity College London exams

2015-2018

Published by:
Trinity College London
www.trinitycollege.com

Registered in the UK
Company no. 02683033
Charity no. 1014792

Printed in Great Britain by Caligraving Ltd.

Minuet in G

Christian Petzold
attrib. J S Bach
arr. Rory Marsden

Tritsch-Tratsch Polka

Johann Strauss II
arr. Jeremy Ward

Voices: Pizz. Strings, Strings
Style: Hip Hop

PLEASE SET UP FOR THE NEXT PIECE

3

The Elephant

from *The Carnival of the Animals*

Camille Saint-Saëns
arr. Nancy Litten

Voices: Cello (sounding octave lower), Strings
Style: Italian Waltz

PLEASE SET UP FOR THE NEXT PIECE

Adiós Muchachos

Sanders
arr. Andrew Smith

Voices: Accordion, Piano
Style: Tango

PLEASE SET UP FOR THE NEXT PIECE

Skye Boat Song

Traditional
arr. Victoria Proudler

Voices: Harp, Pan Flute, Strings
Style: English Waltz

PLEASE SET UP FOR THE NEXT PIECE

El Cóndor Pasa

Daniel Alomía Robles
arr. Andrew Smith

Voice:
Style:

PLEASE SET UP FOR THE NEXT PIECE

The repeat must be played in the examination.

* Candidates should refer to the current syllabus requirements for Own Interpretation pieces.

Yellow Bird

Traditional
arr. Jeremy Ward

Voices: Guitar (sounding octave lower), Pan Flute
Style: Bossanova

PLEASE SET UP FOR THE NEXT PIECE

Perfect Day

Lou Reed
arr. Victoria Proudler

Voices: Alto Saxophone, Strings
Style: ⁶⁄₈ Slow Rock

Theme

from *Dallas*

Jerrold Immel
arr. Joanna Clarke

Voices: Horn, Strings, Synth Lead
Style: Disco

The Homeward Path

Nancy Litten

Voices: Pan Flute, Strings
Style: Ballad

PLEASE SET UP FOR THE NEXT PIECE

Technical Work

Technical work – candidates to prepare in full *either* section i) *or* section ii)					
either **i) Scales & chord knowledge** (from memory) – the examiner will select from the following:					
Bb and D major					
G and B minor (candidate's choice of *either* harmonic *or* melodic *or* natural minor)		two octaves		hands together, unless otherwise stated	piano voice with auto-accompaniment off
Chromatic scale in similar motion starting on Bb	min. ♩ = 80		*legato* and ***mf***		
Pentatonic scale starting on Bb and D (hands separately)		one octave			
A harmonic minor contrary motion scale					
Triad of Bb and D major, G and B minor (root position, first and second inversions)				L.H. only	
Chord of Bb⁷ and D⁷ (root position, first and second inversions)					
or **ii) Exercises** (music may be used):					
Candidates to prepare **all** three exercises.					
The candidate will choose one exercise to play first; the examiner will then select one of the remaining two exercises to be performed.					
Groovy Moves		keyboard functions exercise			
Something Unexpected		scalic exercise			
Strolling		pianistic exercise			

Please refer to the current syllabus for details on all elements of the exam

i) Scales & chord knowledge

Bb major scale (two octaves)

D major scale (two octaves)

G minor scale: harmonic (two octaves)

G minor scale: melodic (two octaves)

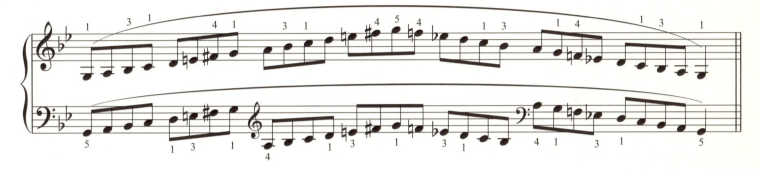

G minor scale: natural (two octaves)

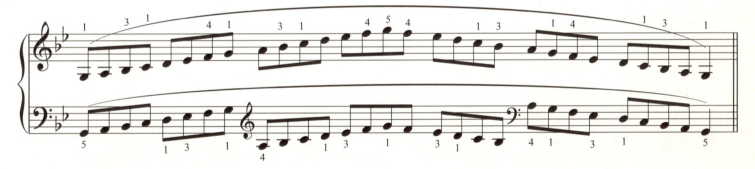

B minor scale: harmonic (two octaves)

B minor scale: melodic (two octaves)

B minor scale: natural (two octaves)

Chromatic scale in similar motion starting on B♭ (one octave)

Pentatonic scale starting on B♭ (one octave)

Right hand

Left hand

Pentatonic scale starting on D (one octave)

Right hand

Left hand

A harmonic minor contrary motion (one octave)

Bb major

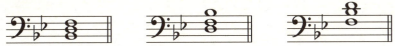

D major

G minor

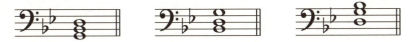

B minor

Bb⁷

D⁷

ii) Exercises

1. Groovy Moves – keyboard functions exercise

Voices: Brass, Saxophone
Style: Big Band *or* Swing

2. Something Unexpected – scalic exercise

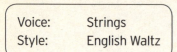

Voice: Strings
Style: English Waltz

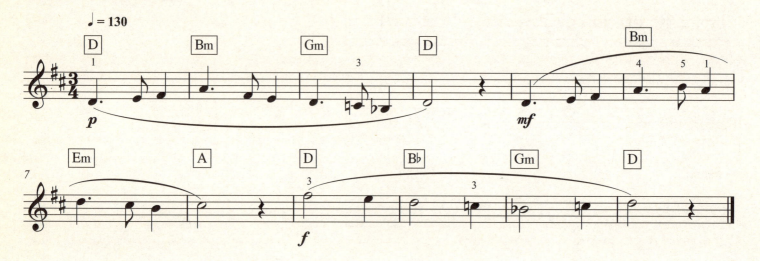

3. Strolling – pianistic exercise

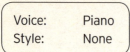

Voice: Piano
Style: None